BLAKE SHELTON

FAMOUS ENTERTAINER

KATIE LAJINESS

Big Buddy Books
An Imprint of Abdo Publishing
abdopublishing.com

BIG BUDDY POP BIOGRAPHIES

abdopublishing.com

Published by Abdo Publishing, a division of ABDO, PO Box 398166, Minneapolis, Minnesota 55439.
Copyright © 2018 by Abdo Consulting Group, Inc. International copyrights reserved in all countries.
No part of this book may be reproduced in any form without written permission from the publisher.
Big Buddy Books™ is a trademark and logo of Abdo Publishing.

Printed in the United States of America, North Mankato, Minnesota.
052017
092017

Cover Photo: Dfree/Shutterstock.com.
Interior Photos: Amy Harris/Invision/AP (p. 25); ASSOCIATED PRESS (pp. 11, 13, 27); Charles Sykes/
    Invision/AP (p. 29); Chris Pizzello/Invision/AP (pp. 6, 19); Evan Agostini/Invision/AP (P. 21);
    ©iStockphoto.com (p. 9); Matt Sayles/Invision/AP (pp. 17, 21); Royce DeGrie/Contributor/Getty
    (p. 23); Sipa USA via AP (p. 5); Vince Bucci/Invision/AP (p. 15); ZUMA Press, Inc./Alamy Stock
    Photo (p. 11).

Coordinating Series Editor: Tamara L. Britton
Graphic Design: Jenny Christensen

Publisher's Cataloging-in-Publication Data

Names: Lajiness, Katie, author.
Title: Blake Shelton / by Katie Lajiness.
Description: Minneapolis, MN : Abdo Publishing, 2018. | Series: Big buddy
    pop biographies | Includes bibliographical references and index.
Identifiers: LCCN 2016962363 | ISBN 9781532110634 (lib. bdg.) |
    ISBN 9781680788488 (ebook)
Subjects: LCSH: Shelton, Blake, 1976- --Juvenile literature. | Country musicians--
    United States--Biography--Juvenile literature. | Singers--United States--
    Biography--Juvenile literature.
Classification: DDC 782.421642092 [B]--dc23
LC record available at http://lccn.loc.gov/2016962363

CONTENTS

COUNTRY SUPERSTAR

Blake Shelton is a talented **performer**, songwriter, and TV star. He is best known for singing country music. Blake has won **awards** for his songs and albums.

With many hit songs, Blake's music has made him famous. He has appeared on magazine covers and popular TV shows.

SNAPSHOT

NAME:
Blake Tollison Shelton

BIRTHDAY:
June 18, 1976

BIRTHPLACE:
Ada, Oklahoma

POPULAR ALBUMS:
Blake Shelton, The Dreamer, Based on a True Story, If I'm Honest

FAMILY TIES

Blake Tollison Shelton was born in Ada, Oklahoma, on June 18, 1976. His parents are Richard and Dorothy Shelton. He has a sister named Endy. When Blake was 14, his half-brother Richie died.

Blake and his former wife Miranda Lambert cowrote the song "Over You" about Blake's brother Richie. It won two song of the year awards.

WHERE IN THE WORLD?

Colorado

Kansas

Missouri

Oklahoma

Arkansas

● Ada

New Mexico

Texas

Louisiana

MEXICO

GULF OF MEXICO

EARLY YEARS

Blake began **performing** at a young age. When he was eight, Blake sang on stage for the first time.

By the time he was in high school, Blake was writing his own songs. In 1992, he won the Denbo Diamond **Award** for young performers in Oklahoma.

After high school, Blake wanted to be a country music singer. So, he moved to Nashville, Tennessee.

Nashville is home to the country music industry. It is known as Music City, USA.

RISING STAR

In Nashville, Blake got a record contract. His first single, "Austin," was a hit. It reached number 18 on the Billboard Hot 100 chart. And, it stayed on the charts for 20 weeks.

In 2001, Blake **released** his first album, *Blake Shelton*. It reached number three on the Billboard Top Country Albums chart. In 2003, Blake toured with country singer Toby Keith.

With the hit song, "Austin," Blake was quickly playing for larger audiences.

In 2004, Blake attended the CMA Awards in Nashville.

Blake's success continued to grow. In 2003, Blake **released** his second album, *The Dreamer*. His song, "The Baby," was a country hit.

Over the next five years, Blake put out three more albums. He followed up each album with a tour across the United States.

People couldn't get enough of Blake. Stories about his life were featured in magazines.

Blake performed at the 2010 CMA Music Festival on June 13, 2010. Later that year, he won Male Vocalist of the Year at the CMA Awards.

COUNTRY FAME

Blake's country music career was on fire. From 2011 to 2014, he **released** three more albums.

In 2016, Blake put out his tenth album. It was called *If I'm Honest*. It reached number one on Billboard's Top Country Albums chart.

Blake won three awards at the 2012 Country Music Awards, including Entertainer of the Year.

TV STAR

Blake is often on TV. He is known for being very funny. In 2015, Blake appeared on *Saturday Night Live* as both an actor and a singer. He sang his hit songs "Boys Round Here" and "Neon Light."

He's been a guest on TV shows such as *The Ellen Degeneres Show* and *TODAY*. On TV, he often talks about his latest album and shares stories about his life.

In 2016, Blake got slimed as he hosted the Kids' Choice Awards.

In 2011, Blake joined *The Voice* as a **coach**. On the show, the coaches **compete** against each other to train a winning singer.

As of 2016, Blake has won five times. This makes him the show's most successful coach.

Blake and *The Voice* coach Gwen Stefani sang "Go Ahead and Break My Heart" at the 2016 Billboard Music Awards.

AWARDS

As a skilled **performer**, Blake is no stranger to **award** shows. Over the years, he has been **nominated** for seven **Grammy Awards**.

In 2011, Blake took home the **CMT Music Award** for Male Video of the Year. The next year, he won **Country Music Association Awards** for **Entertainer** of the Year, Male Vocalist of the Year, and Song of the Year.

In 2013, Blake took home an Academy of Country Music Award. He won Song of the Year for "Over You."

Blake shared the stage with country singer Merle Haggard (left) at the 2014 Grammy Awards.

In 2010, Blake became a member of the **Grand Ole Opry.** Only about 200 **performers** have been asked to join the Opry. Blake was the first singer to be invited on **social media.**

In 2011, Blake cohosted the **Academy of Country Music Awards.** By 2015, he had hosted the show five times and won **awards** four times.

Blake sang at the Grand Ole Opry after he became a member.

GIVING BACK

Blake is known for his generous spirit. He cares about sick children. For his birthday in 2015, Blake asked his fans to give money to a hospital. That year, he also showed support for Red Nose Day. This company helps care for children around the world.

In 2016, Blake sang at the Second Harvest Benefit Concert. This event raised money for a food bank in Tennessee.

OFF THE STAGE

When Blake is not working, he enjoys spending time with friends and family.

Blake lives on a 1,200-acre (486 ha) ranch. It is in Tishomingo, Oklahoma, a town with about 3,000 people. There, Blake hunts and rides all-terrain vehicles.

DID YOU KNOW?
Blake had a pet turkey! The turkey lived at his home in Tennessee.

Blake is an Arizona Cardinals fan. He met football coach Bruce Arians (*right*) in 2015.

BUZZ

Blake continues to be a popular country singer and **entertainer**. In 2017, he will appear on *The Voice* for season 12. And, he is planning a music tour to **perform** songs from *If I'm Honest*. Fans are excited to see what Blake does next!

In 2016, Blake met fans before performing on *TODAY*.

GLOSSARY

Academy of Country Music Awards any of the awards given each year by the Academy of Country Music. These awards seek to improve lives by connecting fans, artists, and the industry.

award something that is given in recognition of good work or a good act.

coach someone who teaches or trains a person or a group on a certain subject or skill.

compete to take part in a contest between two or more persons or groups.

Country Music Association Award any of the awards given each year by the Country Music Association. These awards honor outstanding achievement in the country music industry.

CMT Music Award any of the awards given each year by the Country Music Television station. Winners are chosen by fans who vote online.

entertainer a person who performs for public entertainment.

Grammy Award any of the awards given each year by the National Academy of Recording Arts and Sciences. Grammy Awards honor the year's best accomplishments in music.

Grand Ole Opry a weekly country-music stage concert in Nashville, Tennessee.

nominate to name as a possible winner.

perform to do something in front of an audience. A performer is someone who performs.

release to make available to the public.

social media a form of communication on the Internet where people can share information, messages, and videos. It may include blogs and online groups.

WEBSITES

To learn more about Pop Biographies, visit **abdobooklinks.com**. These links are routinely monitored and updated to provide the most current information available.

INDEX